valentine
50 Songs of Love & Romance

ISBN 978-0-634-05805-9

HAL•LEONARD®
CORPORATION
7777 W. BLUEMOUND RD. P.O. BOX 13819 MILWAUKEE, WI 53213

Visit Hal Leonard Online at
www.halleonard.com

contents

ALL MY LIFE

Words by JOEL HAILEY
Music by JOEL HAILEY and RORY BENNETT

Original key: D♭ major. This edition has been transposed down one half-step to be more playable.

CAN'T HELP FALLING IN LOVE

from the Paramount Picture BLUE HAWAII

Words and Music by GEORGE DAVID WEISS,
HUGO PERETTI and LUIGI CREATORE

ALWAYS AND FOREVER

Words and Music by
ROD TEMPERTON

BOTH TO EACH OTHER
(Friends and Lovers)

Words and Music by PAUL GORDON
and JAY GRUSKA

Medium Ballad

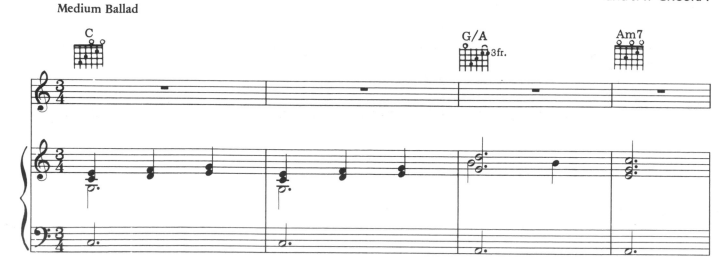

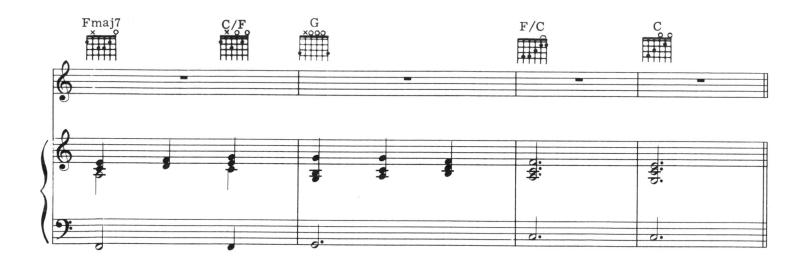

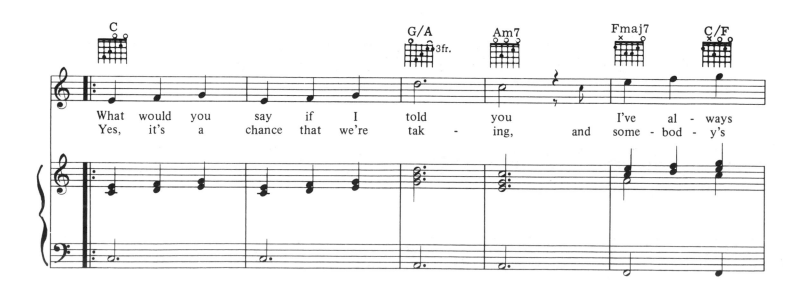

What would you say if I told you, I've al - ways
Yes, it's a chance that we're tak - ing, and some - bod - y's

see. We al - ways know when it's laid on the line, ___ no - bod - y else ___ is as eas - y to find. ___ So I'll oth - er.

D.S. 𝄋 al Coda ⊕

Coda

Can You Feel The Love Tonight

(Pop Version)

from Walt Disney Pictures' THE LION KING
as performed by Elton John

Music by ELTON JOHN
Lyrics by TIM RICE

CAN'T STOP LOVING YOU
(Though I Try)

Words and Music by
BILLY NICHOLLS

DEDICATED TO THE ONE I LOVE

Words and Music by LOWMAN PAULING
and RALPH BASS

CAN'T TAKE MY EYES OFF OF YOU

Words and Music by BOB CREWE
and BOB GAUDIO

Moderately

You're just too good to be true, ____ can't take my eyes off of you. ____ You'd be like
way that I stare, ____ there's noth-ing else to com-pare. ____ The sight of

heav-en to touch, I wan-na hold you so much. At long last
you leaves me weak, there are no words left to speak. But if you

love has ar-rived, and I thank God I'm a-live.
feel like I feel, please let me know that it's real.
You're just too

good to be true, can't take my eyes off of you.
Par-don the

eyes off of you.

DEVOTED TO YOU

Words and Music by
BOUDLEAUX BRYANT

DON'T KNOW MUCH

Words and Music by BARRY MANN,
CYNTHIA WEIL and TOM SNOW

ENDLESS LOVE

from ENDLESS LOVE

Words and Music by
LIONEL RICHIE

Moderately slow

My love, there's on-ly you in my life,
Two hearts, two hearts that beat as one;

the on-ly thing that's right. My
our lives have just be-gun. For-

first love, you're ev-'ry breath that I take,
ev-er, I'll hold you close in my arms,

Oh, _____ and __ love, _____

cresc.

mf

EVERYTHING I HAVE IS YOURS

from the MGM Picture DANCING LADY

Words by HAROLD ADAMSON
Music by BURTON LANE

The more I'm with you, the more I can see— My love is yours a - lone

You came and cap-tured a heart that was free— Now I've noth-ing I can call my own——

Chorus *(slow with expression)*

Eve-ry-thing I Have Is Yours, You're part of me___

Eve-ry-thing I Have Is Yours my des-ti-ny___

I would glad-ly give the sun to you___ If the sun were on-ly mine

I would glad-ly give the earth to you___ and the stars that shine.

Eve-ry-thing that I pos - sess I of - fer you

Let my dream of hap-pi - ness come true

I'd be hap-py just to spend my life Wait - ing at your beck and call

Eve-ry-thing I Have Is Yours my life my all. all.

THE FIRST TIME EVER I SAW YOUR FACE

Words and Music by
EWAN MacCOLL

HEAVEN

Words and Music by BRYAN ADAMS
and JIM VALLANCE

I HONESTLY LOVE YOU

Words and Music by PETER ALLEN
and JEFF BARRY

I JUST CALLED TO SAY I LOVE YOU

Words and Music by
STEVIE WONDER

1. No New Year's Day to cel - e -
rain; no flow - ers
3.,4. (See additional lyrics)

brate; no choc - 'late cov - ered can - dy hearts
bloom; no wed - ding Sat - ur - day __ with - in __

__ to give a - way. __ No first of
__ the month __ of June. __ But what it

Additional Lyrics

3. No summer's high; no warm July;
No harvest moon to light one tender August night.
No autumn breeze; no falling leaves;
Not even time for birds to fly to southern skies.

4. No Libra sun; no Halloween;
No giving thanks to all the Christmas joy you bring.
But what it is, though old so new
To fill your heart like no three words could ever do.
Chorus

I WON'T LAST A DAY WITHOUT YOU

Words and Music by PAUL WILLIAMS
and ROGER NICHOLS

Day af-ter day __ I must face a world __ of strang-ers where I
So man-y times __ when the cit-y seems __ to be with-out a

don't be-long; __ I'm not that strong. It's nice to know __ that there's
friend-ly face, __ a lone-ly place, it's nice to know __ that you'll

some-one I __ can turn to who will al-ways care; __ you're
be there if __ I need you, and you'll al-ways smile; __ it's

JUST THE WAY YOU ARE

Words and Music by
BILLY JOEL

I'LL HAVE TO SAY I LOVE YOU IN A SONG

Words and Music by
JIM CROCE

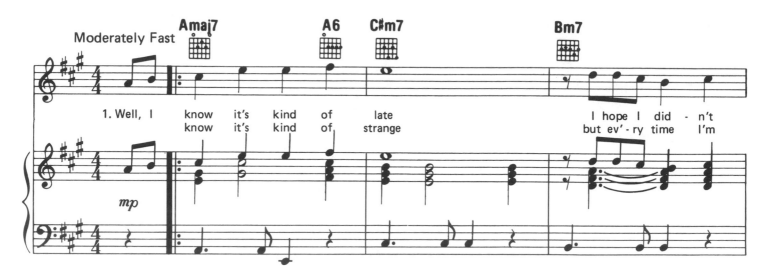

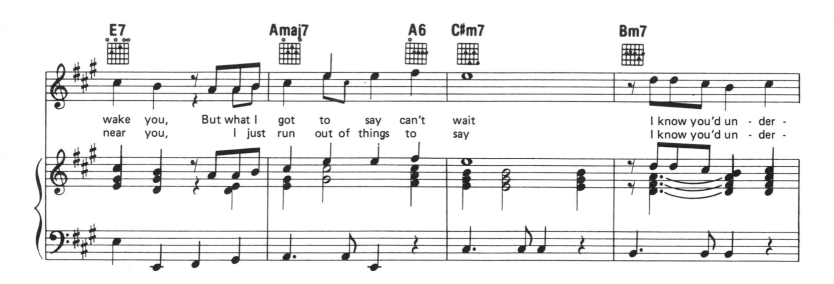

IF

Moderately, with feeling

Words and Music by
DAVID GATES

pic - ture paints a thou - sand words, _ then why _

man could be two plac - es at _ one time, _

L-O-V-E

Words and Music by BERT KAEMPFERT
and MILT GABLER

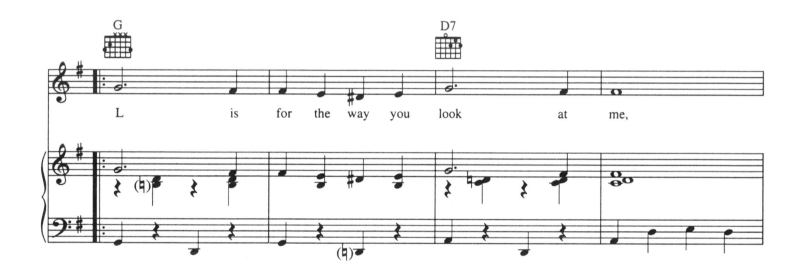

L is for the way you look at me,

O is for the on-ly one I see.

V is ver - y, ver - y ex - tra - or - di - na - ry.

E is e - ven more than an - y - one that you a - dore can.

Love is all that I can give to you.

Love is more than just a game for two.

LESSONS LEARNED

Words and Music by
DAN FOGELBERG

Moderate (easy rock)

1. You, with the past at your back and the fu-ture un-sure,
2. Me, in a sea of con-fu-sion, drift-in' with the tide,

asked for the chance to try love once
liv - ing on love that had long since

LADY IN RED

Words and Music by
CHRIS DeBURGH

Moderately slow

LIGHT MY FIRE

Words and Music by
THE DOORS

LOVE SONG

Words and Music by
LESLEY DUNCAN

The words_ I have to say _ may well _ be
You say_ it's ver-y hard _ to leave _ be -

sim - ple but they're true.
hind the life we knew.

MONA LISA

from the Paramount Picture CAPTAIN CAREY, U.S.A.

Words and Music by JAY LIVINGSTON
and RAY EVANS

MY FUNNY VALENTINE
from BABES IN ARMS

Words by LORENZ HART
Music by RICHARD RODGERS

MY HEART WILL GO ON
(Love Theme from 'Titanic')
from the Paramount and Twentieth Century Fox Motion Picture TITANIC

Music by JAMES HORNER
Lyric by WILL JENNINGS

Ev - 'ry night in my dreams I see you, I feel you, that is how I know you go on.

NEVER GONNA LET YOU GO

Words and Music by BARRY MANN
and CYNTHIA WEIL

swear this time, __ I'm nev - er gon - na let you go. ___

Instrumental solo

NOW AND FOREVER
(You and Me)

Words and Music by JIM VALLANCE,
RANDY GOODRUM and DAVID FOSTER

Moderately slow Rock

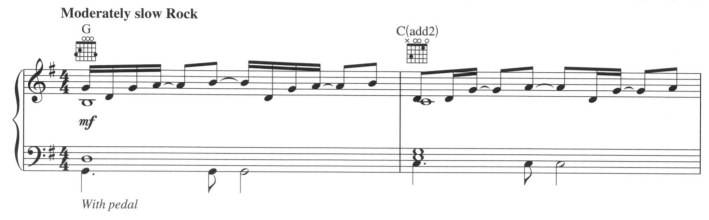

With pedal

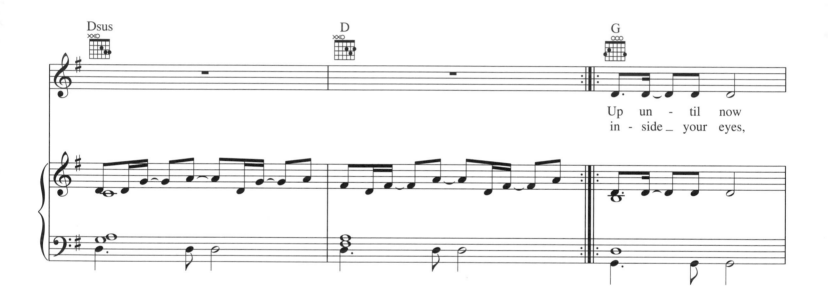

Up un - til now
in - side_ your eyes,

I've learned to live_ with - out love,
I can see mys - ter - ies there.

You and me, we've got a des-ti-ny. Start-ing to-night,

we'll be to-geth-er.

You and me, this is what love should be, and it's gon-na be right,

Repeat and Fade

Optional Ending

now and for-ev-er.

ON THE WINGS OF LOVE

Words and Music by JEFFREY OSBORNE
and PETER SCHLESS

Just smile __ for me __ and let __ the day __ be-gin. __
You look __ at me __ and I __ be-gin __ to melt __

You are __ the sun-shine __ that lights my heart __ with-in. __
just like __ the snow when __ a ray of sun __ is felt. __

and I'm yours__ ex - clu - sive - ly.___ And right now___ we live__ and

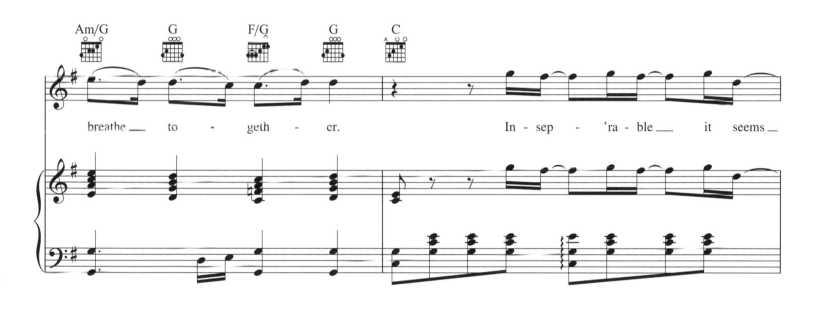

breathe __ to - geth - er. In - sep - 'ra - ble __ it seems__

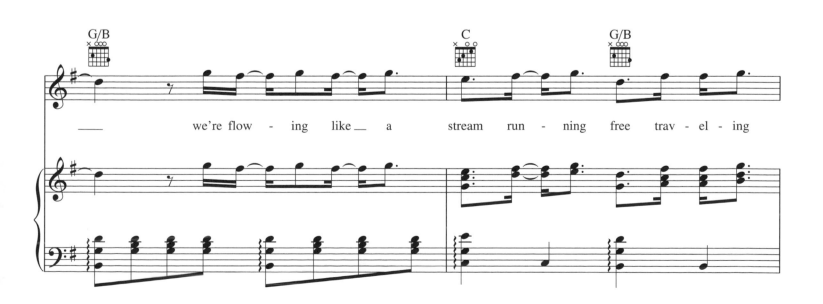

___ we're flow - ing like __ a stream run - ning free trav - el - ing

ONE IN A MILLION YOU

Words and Music by
SAM DEES

Love had played its games on me so long I start-ed to be-lieve I'd nev-er find an-y-one. Doubt had tried

A♭13 A♭7 B♭/F F♯dim
and oh, what a rev - e - la - tion to
Gm7 Cm7
see some - one was say - ing, "I love you" to me.
E♭/F B♭ B♭maj9
A one in a mil - lion,
B♭7 A♭/C B♭7/D E♭maj7 A♭13 A♭7
chance of a life - time. And life showed com -

SHE LOVES YOU

Words and Music by JOHN LENNON
and PAUL McCARTNEY

She loves you, yeah, yeah, yeah— She loves you, yeah,

yeah, yeah,— She loves you, yeah, yeah, yeah,

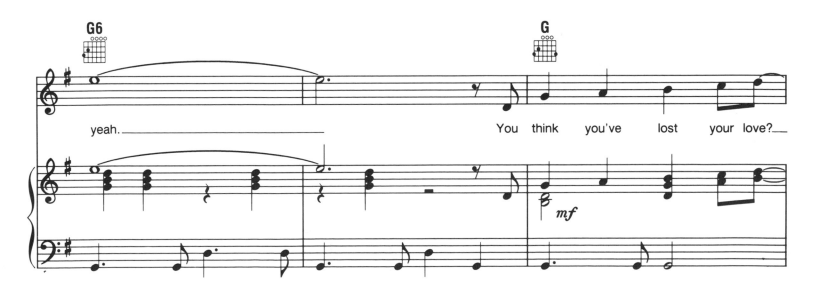

yeah.___ You think you've lost your love?___

SOMETHING

Words and Music by
GEORGE HARRISON

Some - thing in ___ the way ___ she moves, ___
Some - where in ___ her smile ___ she knows, ___
Some - thing in ___ the way ___ she knows, ___

at - tracts ___ me like ___ no oth - er lov - er.
that I ___ don't need ___ no oth - er lov - er.
and all ___ I have ___ to do is think ___ of her.

Some - thing in ___ the way ___ she woos ___ me. ___
Some - thing in ___ her style ___ that shows ___ me. ___
Some - thing in ___ the things ___ she shows ___ me. ___

I don't want to leave her now,   you

SOMEWHERE ALONG THE WAY

Words by SAMMY GALLOP
Music by KURT ADAMS

(You're My)
SOUL AND INSPIRATION

Words and Music by BARRY MANN
and CYNTHIA WEIL

THREE COINS IN THE FOUNTAIN

from THREE COINS IN THE FOUNTAIN

Words by SAMMY CAHN
Music by JULE STYNE

Three coins in the foun - tain, each one seek - ing hap - pi -

ness, thrown by three hope - ful lov - ers, which one will the foun - tain

bless? Three hearts in the foun - tain,

TONIGHT, I CELEBRATE MY LOVE

Music by MICHAEL MASSER
Lyric by GERRY GOFFIN

Slowly and expressively

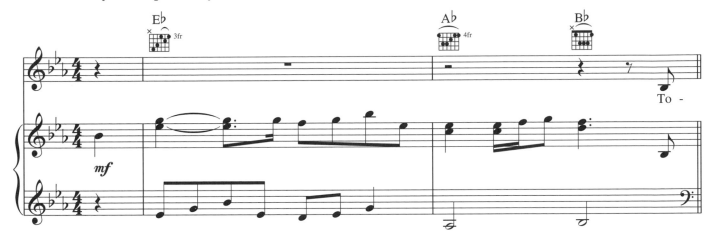

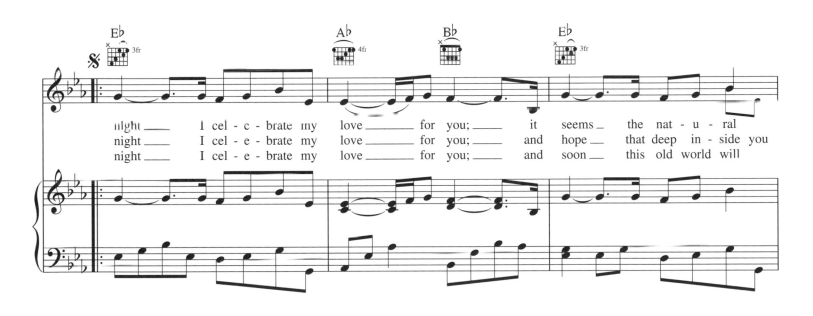

night ___ I cel-e-brate my love ___ for you; ___ it seems ___ the nat-u-ral
night ___ I cel-e-brate my love ___ for you; ___ and hope ___ that deep in-side you
night ___ I cel-e-brate my love ___ for you; ___ and soon ___ this old world will

thing ___ to do.   To-night   no one's gon-na   find us, ___ we'll leave the world be-
feel ___ it too.   To-night ___ our spir-its will be climb-ing to   a   sky lit up ___ with
seem ___ brand new.   To-night   we will both dis-cov-er ___ how friends turn in-to

TONIGHT I FELL IN LOVE

Words and Music by MARGO,
MARGO, MEDRESS and SIEGAL

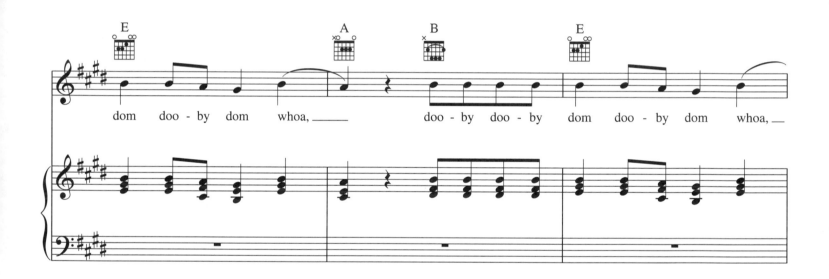

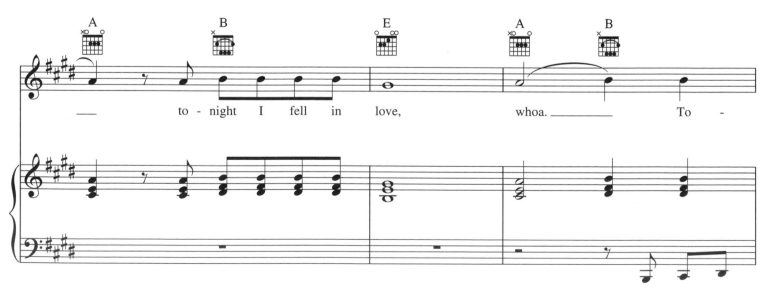

WE'VE ONLY JUST BEGUN

Words and Music by ROGER NICHOLS
and PAUL WILLIAMS

Slowly

We've on-ly just be-gun ___ to live. ___

___ White lace and prom - i - ses, a kiss for luck _ and we're

on our way. ___

(1.) Be - fore the ris - ing
(2.,D.S.) And when the eve - ning

THE TWELFTH OF NEVER

Words by PAUL FRANCIS WEBSTER
Music by JERRY LIVINGSTON

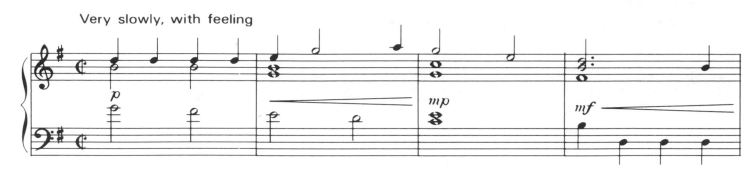

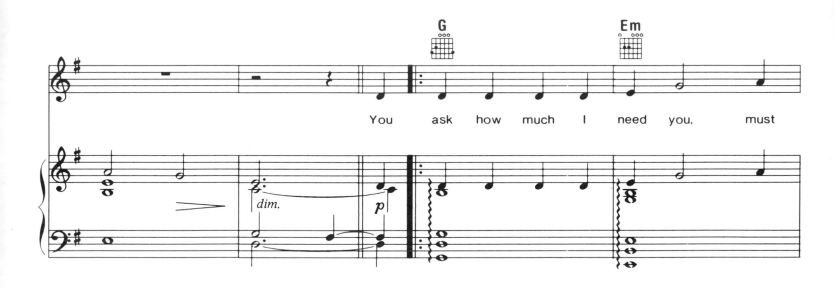

You ask how much I need you, must

I ex - plain? I need you, oh, my dar - ling, like

VALENTINE

Words and Music by JACK KUGELL
and JIM BRICKMAN

If there were no words, ___ no way to speak, ___ I ___

All of my life, ___ I have been wait - ing for ___ all

___ would still ___ hear ___ you. ___ If there were no tears, ___ no way to feel ___

___ you give ___ to ___ me. ___ You've o - pened my eyes ___ and shown me how ___

WHEN LOVE IS ALL THERE IS
(Wedding Story)
Theme from TLC's A WEDDING STORY

Music and Lyrics by
CHRIS CURTIS

When love is all there is, you don't re-mem-ber the mo-ments when you have-n't seen her face, and some-thing in your heart makes you sur-ren-der _____ to a feel-ing that your dreams could not re-place. When

YEARS FROM NOW

Words and Music by ROGER COOK
and CHARLES COCHRAN

YOU AND ME AGAINST THE WORLD

Words and Music by PAUL WILLIAMS
and KEN ASCHER

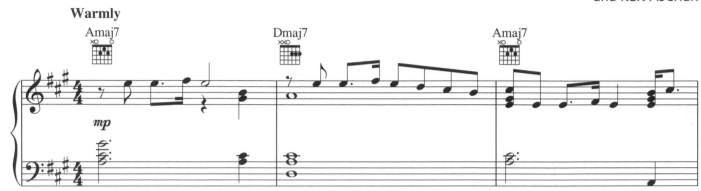

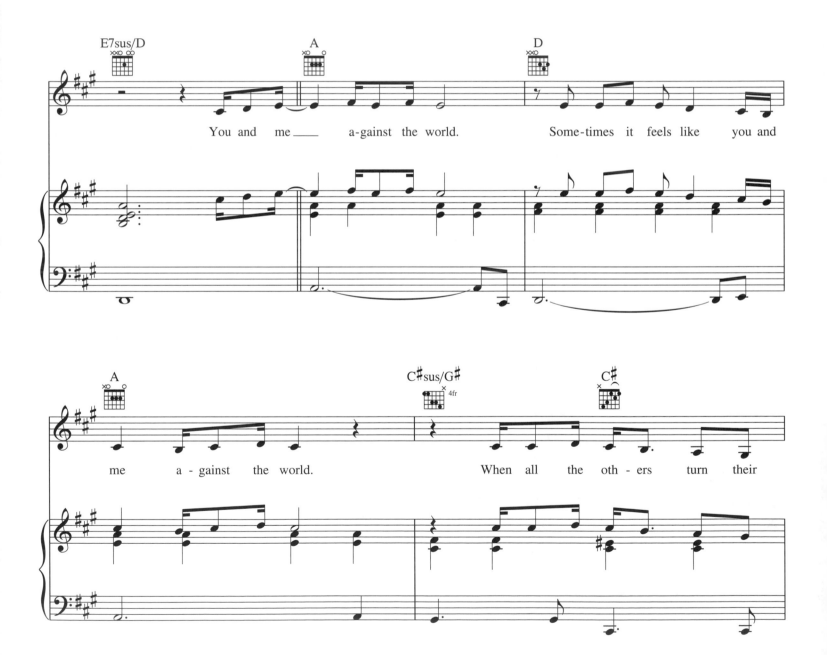

YOU ARE SO BEAUTIFUL

Words and Music by BILLY PRESTON
and BRUCE FISHER

YOU ARE THE SUNSHINE OF MY LIFE

Words and Music by
STEVIE WONDER

YOU'LL ACCOMP'NY ME

Words and Music by
BOB SEGER

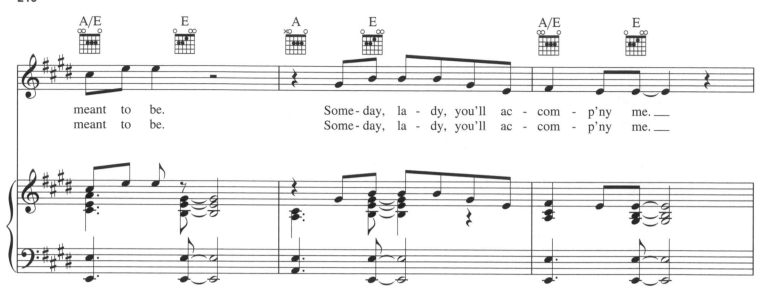

meant to be.　　Some-day, la - dy, you'll ac - com - p'ny me. ___
meant to be.　　Some-day, la - dy, you'll ac - com - p'ny me. ___

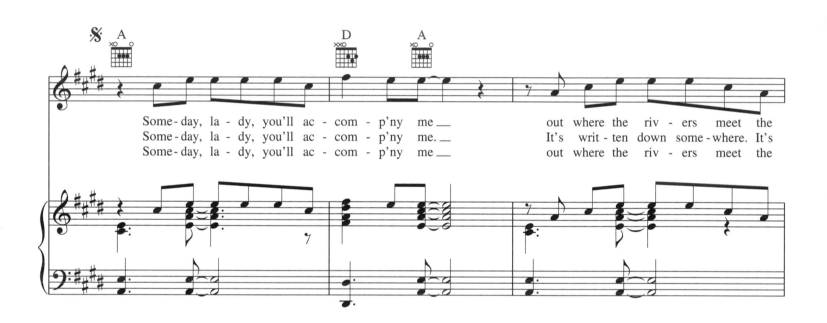

Some-day, la - dy, you'll ac - com - p'ny me ___　out where the riv - ers meet the
Some-day, la - dy, you'll ac - com - p'ny me. ___　It's writ - ten down some - where. It's
Some-day, la - dy, you'll ac - com - p'ny me ___　out where the riv - ers meet the

sound - ing sea. ___　You're high a - bove me now. You're
got ___ to be. ___　You're high a - bove me, fly - ing
sound - ing sea. ___　I feel it in my soul. It's

YOU'VE GOT A FRIEND

Words and Music by
CAROLE KING

*Vocal harmony sung 2nd time only

You've Made Me So Very Happy

Words and Music by BERRY GORDY, FRANK E. WILSON,
BRENDA HOLLOWAY and PATRICE HOLLOWAY

I lost at love __ be- fore, got mad and closed __ the door, _____ but you said try just once more. I chose you for the one, __ now I'm hav-ing so much fun.